This book belongs to:

Name: _____

Date: _____

Contact: _____

_____

Cover art: 'Red Fern' by Hannah Parker, 12.
Published in *Stone Soup* Magazine, June 2018.

Stone Soup, founded in 1973, is published by Children's Art Foundation—Stone Soup Inc., a nonprofit organization based in the Unted States. Find out more at Stonesoup.com.

StoneSoup

www.ingramcontent.com/pod-product-compliance
Lightning Source LLC
Chambersburg PA
CBHW072007290426
44109CB00018B/2158